Night Horses

Linda Rose Parkes

Night Horses

Hearing Eye

Published by Hearing Eye 2010

Hearing Eye, Box 1, 99 Torriano Avenue
London NW5 2RX, UK
email: hearing_eye@torriano.org
for book orders: books@hearingeye.org

www.hearingeye.org

Poems © Linda Rose Parkes, 2010

ISBN: 978-1-905082-58-2

Acknowledgements are due to the editors of the following:
Ambit, The Interpreter's House, Iota, Dream Catcher,
Amnesty International 'Poets Against War,'
Second Light live, Artemis, Leaf Garden Press,
Poetry tREnD English-German translation.

The poem 'The Tree' was commissioned by
The Jersey Sculpture Trust
and is inscribed at the foot of a sculpture
created by Richard Perry
on the waterfront in St Helier.

Hearing Eye is represented by
Inpress Ltd in the UK – see www.inpressbooks.co.uk
Trade distribution:
Central Books, Hackney Wick, London E9 5LN

Printed and bound by Imprintdigital.net
Cover photograph by Martin Parker
Designed by Martin Parker at www.silbercow.co.uk

Contents

Gift	9
Wading in	10
The narrative build	11
Casket	12
I had a crush on Bronco Lane so	
decided to write us together	14
Girl on a mountain pass	15
Dawdling boy picks up momentum	16
Swimming out	18
The solicitude of friends	20
L'amitié	21
Orphanage	22
The high speed train	23
Ghost ladder	24
Late back from leave	25
The U-boat Kapitän summoned by Pegasus	26
Jüngchen	28
The White Witch	29
On the eve of radium	35
Marie Curie travels to the Front	36
Marie Curie, in her last days,	
listens to Madame Butterfly	37
Chasing tides	38
My mother, sheltering	39
My mother on the back of my chariot	40
My mother's courage tape	42
The broomcycle	43
Lair	44
Dance to your daddie	45
Whenever the van pulls up	46
The upholstered stage	47
Hello Daddy	48
Slippage	49

The blown nest	50
The seasoned dancer	51
The longest hold	52
The word for father	53
A night scene	55
A sex doll	56
If on the stairs	57
The tree	58
The angel	59
Terra Nova II	61
Horse queen	62
Bray	63
Talking the cat to the vet	64
Angel ascending	65
A pair of socks	66
A stack of blue-glazed bowls	67
The sliding hills	68
Muses of the shower room	69

*for Michael
and for
Esther, Samuel and Becca*

*with special thanks to Susan Johns for her
commitment and scrupulous editing skills
and in grateful memory of John Rety.*

Gift

A black mare inhabits your stable
with its bales of hay,
cool, clean pails of water,
dry sacks of feed.
She is in your keeping.

In daylight you lead her to the field
with a beech tree for shelter;
the sun flares like tinder
in the swish of her tail,
her glimmering hooves.

Each evening you ride the bridle paths
down to the sea: canter, now gallop, at the edge
of the waves unfurling as the spumy moon rises,
billowing her mane.

Then something in the air begins to slide;
in ways you don't notice the weather has turned,
the light in the wind wanes, grows sluggish,
the tide dims, the moon falters – there's a slackness
in the reins, a loosening

of the taut rhythms that hold your span of inspiration,
the fleetness slowing like the end of love
which entrusted you with this fabled creature

tethered now
without food or water.

Suddenly your sleep gusts open:
and even before you lunge out of bed –
even before you are fully awake –
you are running for the stable ...
running to the black mare ...

Wading in

His keen and easy movements belonged to a surfer
hitching his board on an old van,
making for the swell, mid-winter,
kestrels hovering above the caves.

But in the nine-to-five, when he tried to haul
onto his boss's truck too many boxes
at once, they all careened
to the pavement,

while I – spurred by the tow inside him – urged my pen
towards the headlands of silence and thrift, gliding
seabirds. Cliffs reared out
of washed sand, waves lit up, were held

suspended in the instant before their perfect
spill, when the last slack
coil of the dream
surges.

Every moment spent chasing cardboard,
the steadfast page waits for him.

The narrative build

Perhaps if we'd known what they had for breakfast
(an underdone egg, a clip on the ear?)
we'd have guessed in time they weren't to be toyed with,
two boys minding their own conversation
and sloping by up the lane –

    Oi! Sideburns!
    and your mate!
    we taunted from behind the fence ...

        and then –
            their boots bludgeoning the steps
              the rasp of the gate forced
        open – us running
        harder than our years could carry
    for the unlatched door ...

Why is it their shadows now stain the path?
their blank height, their occluding eyes
outline a warning: a far-reaching absence
of signs etched on leaves or glass
which would allow me to read

        the sudden warp
        of intention,
            the direction of the wind
              spiralling
            through the trees,
              snatching chance strands
            then weaving them
              into hard narrative.

Casket

Of how she came upon the place
after hazardous journeying
under black cloud,
narrow-steep and darkling
lanes –
    is a thread
unwinding to the place
that ushered her
in at the top of the cliffs
booming with waves.
        A polished spoon
held a mirror to her face,
floating above a white cloth.
And whenever she put food to her mouth,
    there were ravens,
in vigil, circling,
knowing she'd unravel
the path,
    a fairy child wanting
for a bowl of kindness.
And every adult
in the palace opened to her
something like love.

But how to recall the voices of the wind
swishing the firs,
      for one cocooned
at the heart of a tale,
who doesn't remember
she was there? although,
sometimes,
      when she shuts her eyes –
murmurings
from a veiled banquet ...
      And when ocean
lashes the sky
in gusts,
      gleanings
of hope rise
from a hidden casket.

**I had a crush on Bronco Lane
so decided to write us together**

Naked to the waist, prospecting for gold, wheeling in his lean barrow
the kissed-by-stardust, ethereal girl nobody could touch

without my say-so. He was always ready to ignore the script,
lift her to his mouth, his bow of salt music. My task was to stall him

with my ploy of words which would never tire of trying to compose
her beauty. His rapture must not ebb

through a lull in the text, the kiss denouement. I had no inkling
of how love persists, traipsing across the same town

or facing down cold: how in crooked windows of plain streets,
people kiss on. No sense that Bronco might gaze beyond

her skin to wonder at the marvels beating there. That *she* might press him
to *her* breast or strike out solo. What I floated was bliss,

its anticipation, a gossamer moon poised on the horizon. Each night
I built their longing fresh, safe from the ruin of disappointment.

Not for them a life of hens, kids or troublesome neighbours
pegging out wash and gossiping full-throat. Their lips would hover

but would never crush – he'd wait forever
if I said he should, for the valley of the buried gold.

Girl on a mountain pass

And my child's companion became form,
pungent with goat smell, humming
with goat noise,

he nuzzled her sleeve,
play-butted her palm,
she stroking his chin, his high neck.

How many jumpers could we knit from his yarn,
his black lustrous fleece of angel's hair?

But even as she slips
into the crags of his eyes,
they each answer in their own voice:

his, the sounds of Quechua carrying on the air
and spun again
in goat meaning,

hers, the child-woman threaded
with beads of pain scattering
as she climbs beyond reach

of the mountain pass
to where his softly padding herd
eddies the wild seeds.

Dawdling boy
picks up
momentum

for Samuel

Knees splayed under low-slung handlebars
    his gangly, calf-like limbs bridled –
the pent-up grace
    of a boy who lists
when he walks

Half-hidden behind a wildflower bank
    a cow reared her head
and made to kiss him
    he veered –
        nearly lost
    balance
righted himself
on his short saddle …
    the elegance of the near thing

She'd heard him of course
    the ticking of his wheels
in her nasal world could sniff
    his presence, the sweet-warm sweat
of young skin – her calf
    not full-weaned
from her wet-lick
    corralling tongue

But the calf
    cycles on
      pedalling faster
       now faster
racing himself
      against
        himself past the flood-green
   fields, the leafing
trees holding the bend
   boy
      as boy
         propelled
by space and time

      her eyes still following

Swimming out

for Carole

No, it wasn't wise to strip off,
give herself over
to the waves slapping
her knees and then her breasts
before she lunged
into the steeply
shelving ocean
in late summer's emptied bay
where the kiosk
flapped its ripped
awning and the slipway
merged into the hill
studded with conifers
and crumbling cliff.

But so often the wind
had pummelled her windows
and salt stained the glass. Now finally
she was pushing out
from a paint-flaked,
middle-aging house
of dust-scorched roses.
If she made it beyond
the hook of fear,
success would surf her
past the lowering
rocks and if her strokes
stalled she'd learn to float
until the creases in her breath

dissolved and it was only
the brine in her veins
which owned her –
her spirit rising
like Leviathan,
*eyes like eyelids
of the morning.*

The solicitude of friends

for Julia

I was looking for the rock which stubbed your foot,
scanning where I thought the tide-line was that summer

we made our way from town, thirsty for blue nuanced
only by the line of the horizon. A blackened jetty marked the spot

we dumped our clothes. I don't know if you know
how much I think about you ferrying me year in, year out,

never missing a gig. About how once while I slept
in your spare room, you dreamed you couldn't reach

the notes, stood there at the mike in front of strangers,
dressed in a threadbare, flimsy raiment fit for the wash,

wishing you'd replaced the missing buttons, repaired the seams
frayed on both sides, a garment of failure worn inside out.

Now I train my attention on that ridge until it dissolves
into this winter afternoon of sanderlings feeding at the flow's

edge. And the sky – we wear it, don't we, in our heads?
these rolls of fabric, this breeze-blue

drift which after each bad day has silently unfurled,
more flared with light, more resplendent. Kinder.

L'amitié

A tumbril sways along the Quai de Louvre,
Danton propping up Camille, who's grieving

for his one true wife, who would step up
to the guillotine alone the following week.

The cart jolts. How not to faint or fall into betrayal
as they're shuffling back the collar to bare the neck?

What if I were Danton – but in my woman's togs …
could I hold you to the end where the tumbril halts

at the iron-swilled stench of La Place de la Revolution?
Instead, we place our order in the shade

of a plane tree in Le Marais: this coffee as good
as I have ever tasted.

Nous, deux amies …
what will be our test?

And again I glimpse them:
Danton with his arms around Camille.

Surely the executioner thought of deserting the blade,
brought face to face with such communion?

Their hair's been shorn – Camille, his curls –
their shirts ripped at the elbows, under the arms;

impossible to escape that sound,
the shadowy tumbril lurching

over the cobbles, past the old houses,
wheels clattering.

Orphanage

Can you see the outline of a six year old,
hovering in the doorway,
post war?

Her gaze wolfs the slices of white bread,
buttered and laid out with the laundered
serviettes for dignitaries and local benefactors.

Does she dare steal a triangle?

Shadows trail her silhouette:
her monthly ration will be docked for a year –
she'll watch the rows of other children,

taste it melting on their tongues like the sunlight
dancing on trestle tables.

Butter's the thing she craves,
the tenuous door
to her mother's kisses,

to her father taking off his black felt hat,
swishing her up onto his wide-brimmed shoulders.

Will there be left-over crusts
of half-moon bites?

She'll cram the first piece in her mouth. Then another.
And another.

The high speed train

Shouldn't something have brushed her sleeve?
the tingle of a Wim Wenders angel
holding her back from the *might be*,
steadying her to the *what is*.

In a tunnel of mulched leaves
or on a dead-end platform,
is not love always there?

Having just been told we'd lost a stranger,
we filed from the carriages at Vitres
like mourners, in need of a drink,
somewhere to sit out the wreckage
of stop.

But the air keened, hung over the station,
the static of someone
who had not quite left, hesitating
on the verge
of our senses.

Ghost ladder

*I could see the gas works
through the reek of hops
from the nearby brewery …
in my head I climb the breathing drum
that dwarfs the terraces,
gauge the depth,
the tread distance.
But the moment I heave
myself onto the rim,
I plummet through the smoke
and shadow.*

Years on, the story of a boy
bullied into climbing
a disused gas holder,
hauling himself up
the rust-crazed steps,
feet skidding on black moon-frost,
face ashen-old,
his hands and knees ripping.

Had nothing readied him for this?
no pretend-scaling
the mind's gradient –
no Apelles line, no ghost ladder –
prepared him for the absence
of the two last rungs,
the jeering voices
sauntering
away?

Late back from leave

The sun hung upside down
in the fruit tree, licking the skins
of young pears.
His mother poured a *Tasse Kaffee*
strong enough to stand up a spoon,
called for him to come to breakfast:
three months into Stalingrad.
Three times she called;
he couldn't bring himself
to turn from the window,
transfixed by leaves criss-crossing the grass,
the beads of fruit glistering with dew.

Had she known how much danger
was mounting,
she'd have frog-marched him,
on time, to the station.
Instead she walked quietly upstairs,
and standing beside him,
tried to fix her gaze
on the same things. The leaves
on the grass, the lush fruit.

There's no record of how long they stood,
whether they ran to catch the train,
or decided he should go the next day
with a letter apologising
to the Kommandant.
She was in the garden,
fingers stained with blackcurrants,
when they led him to the wall
and tied the blindfold.

The U-boat Kapitän summoned by Pegasus

Every night I was looking for a sign
that I could sleep without dreams
of broken men – I watched the enemy

captain stroll on the bridge, a streak
of bubbles tracking the torpedo,
stokers, grooms storming the hatchways,

and wedged stall upon stall,
the rearing, slipping horses
bound for the Front.

I crammed my eyes with stars
in the hope of a day worth the trouble
of my ablutions, the wearing of a good tie.

But stranded nightly in my backyard,
I was summoned by ghosts:
the bay mare quivering

in the horse star constellation,
the lunging deeps of her eyes
as she attempted to swim,

the white stallion leaping
over the berthing rail –
when I saw him land – *oh mein gott!*

in a full-laden boat, I shut down
the periscope,
shouted orders to dive.

Finally run aground, in slippers and bathrobe,
I kneel to Pegasus, under the weight
of what I've done. Tonight,

inside the whinnying dark,
gashing hooves, veering flanks,
sweeping necks of arched muscle

come to perfect rest. And lifting
from the blood and smoke,
the mangled souls rise.

Jüngchen

after 'The Reader' by Bernhard Schlink

The boy was fifteen when he met Hanna, who was 36.
Only during her trial years later, did he discover
she'd been an S.S. guard and that she was illiterate.

She called me *Rose, Pebble, Frog* …
    What animal was she?
Powerful flanks bristling with muscles,
    smooth sheeny skin,
      I named her *Horse*,
Cheval if she preferred
      or *Little Equus* …

This time, quietly, she led
the horse word from the stable,
    freeing it from halter and rein,
watched as it cantered
      in the open
    tossing its mane –
      a winged creature.

And there's always a blue dress
when I shut my eyes,
    bike tracks running
through the forest,
    her two hands gripping
      upright handlebars –

me so afraid her skirt would catch
    in the wheels – that gust of blue
  whipped like loose awning
or a half-hoisted sail,
    her thin cloth shuddering
      towards language.

The White Witch

Maria Sibylla Merian, born in 1647, Frankfurt, botanical artist and entomologist

i *A Cabinet of Curiosities*

Frankfurt, 1647. The plague over.
Frau Merian could no longer
tie her apron in her seventh month,

but still rolled up her sleeves –
her heart burnished by hygiene
and thrift – filled a pail, intending
to scour the cupboard.

But what hoard of treasure on opening the door!
Molluscs, fluted, star-sprigged
flowers … and, spinning a rapture of fine dust,
the luminous spread wings
of pinned butterflies.

How many times (she shuddered
to recall) did she embrace the radiance
of earth, sea and air?
unable to throw any one thing away.

Her daughter Maria,
crouched in the womb,
absorbing the covenant from the placenta,

would from the age of nine
be pricking air holes
into boxes and jars.

ii Tulip thief, 1656

But soon the neighbour came drumming up our stairs
in his leather boots, behind my mother,
to the attic where I'd set up my easel.

I'd picked only the one half-open tulip,
white blushed vermilion against black stamens.
His bulb had cost two thousand marks.

"Still, I'm not a cruel man: recompense enough,
this painting's likeness."

What pleased him was its invisible window
where the sky seeped in,
tight but breezy with hidden storms

of insects; he swore if he cupped his ear
to the canvas he could hear – inside the crisp petals –
a lightning swarm of careful brush-strokes.

iii A dangerous profession for a woman

Talk to me, Maria,
   in the mirror,
your horse face shining
   as you brush your hair.
Tell me about
   your flaky marriage,
strapped for cash
   with two little girls,
your shelves stacked
   with oil, brandy,
candles and boxes
   of glittering needles:
your mother's torment
   at you grubbing around
for *beasts of the devil* –
   women burned
at the stake for less.

Talk to me, Maria,
   about loneliness,
journeying so far
   into the dark
until growth splits
   its strange cocoon …
three thousand metres
   of white thread
wrapped around
   a tiny worm
is the silk which spins
   a patient voice,
you who wove
   yourself with such
finesse – your husk
   dissolving
in air
   and light –
wings emerging,
   a *White Witch*
      flying out.

iv Cabin fever

*Seventeen year old Dorothea travels with her
mother Maria to Surinam, where they will collect
samples and make sketches in the rainforest.*

What had we learned after three months
of breathing the shadows of sails,
in airless quarters, under heavy rigging?

A daughter and her fifty two year old mother
on their way to Surinam. Of course there were squalls
about how a woman should behave on deck
or at the captain's table.

And I'd never noticed, before, the colour
of that impartial gaze at full
beam, how she clicked her tongue
in that fiercely absorbed way.

But so much happens in the margins,
in the ghostly scrawl outside the page;
the wiping of sickness from each other's face,
the back chat, chidings, rinsing undies.

How often did we wince at the cost of the journey,
brace ourselves with prayer when we thought we were
lost to the perilous waves – swelling bigger, now blacker.

v Bees and wasps flew in our faces

*Maria and Dorothea worked for two years
in the rainforest, returning only when
Maria became critically ill with malaria.*

We struggled like two foolish Mädchen
in the long cotton layers
of our masquerading skirts.

The slaves, who used the *flos pavonis*
to abort their slave children,
cut us a path through the luxuriance
of the forest, brought us vanilla pods
and mussels, chilli peppers crushed on bread
while we sketched the white bulb
of the red amaryllis, costumes
of butterflies and moths,
the camouflage of their cocoons
like lumps of turd
and fat raindrops.

vi Hinterland

Some say it started with a father's voice,
fluttering inside her three year old head:
his daughter would be someone ...

But let's abandon daughter trying to please
dad and lift the lid on that chaotic space
of memory and dream
which can't be read except
in shadows steeping a volcanic lake
or shielding the north face
of an unbidden tale.

What is it that consigns us
to a place, a hinterland
where no one else is storming
the air and raking light,
with the exact same
demons, the same blade of love?

On the eve of radium

After months and months of Pierre
and his electrometer,
the stink of soda and acids,
I slipped out the house
to indulge in a coveted café crème.

But each time I blinked our girls
grew taller ...
hearts lit behind the bone,
loops and fissures of their brains
tracing delicate pathways.

So I chose one red and one blue-
beaded hairpin, was quickening
my pace – urgency
suddenly fulminating
to be home in the lab ...

when, *merde, alors!* I'd left the gifts
on the counter ... forced myself to turn
back into the boulevard, the spark
on my girls' illumined faces vying
with the glow of the sheened glass vats.

Marie Curie travels to the Front

What to pack in the lorry with the x-ray
equipment? Blankets, of course. Soap.
Tinned soup? Apples?

Irene, her eldest, braced for ditches and bends,
is napping fitfully ... Marie still fearful
of her own judgment in allowing her to come.
The technician silent at the wheel.

Was Marie gazing out the window at a wave of light
shuddering through the grass: memory darting
to its burrow, the blind, startled instinct of a hare?

Were there moments when she spiralled
backwards to Pierre and the shaded
corner of the garden where the sun tipped
into the row of yews? before she pulled her thoughts up

sharp for trying to ward off the present,
a present beyond controlled
experiment and every measure of failure
or succour of discipline.

Mutinous, she marshals the promise to take their work
to the Front Line
        and the lorry stutters
           changes gear
                    rolls forward ...

Marie Curie, in her last days, listens to Madame Butterfly

After so much humming in the chorus,
how could the geisha *not* love
faithless Pinkerton? his glance

so freighted with chemistry and hormones,
she was bound to break into strange pieces
and be borne through the hoops
of the diva's stringent art –

vowels, phrasing, the burnishing C
which penetrates the bone like light –
carries the spirit beyond pain.

Ah, the rapture of the vocal line,
if it could but hold me ...
become my alchemist,
the fioritura of ocean and stars.

Chasing tides

Pulling on that rubber cap of turquoise petals,
tamping threads of stray hair –
you were never a serious swimmer
who strikes out beyond the bay,

shadow skimming mackerel, conger eels.
But you gave your daughters a hankering for sea
which has us to this day chasing the tide.

Now we coax you up to your ankles,
even mid-thigh; place your chair
where waves eddy the forsaken shapes
of who we were as they glide
below the puckering surface.

Once, on a spring tide,
the salt hills keening challenge,
sun already peaked –
our strokes still vigorous enough
to push the density of water,
we clutched your arm –

the rip of the next swell
about to take you.

My mother, sheltering

Suddenly you lose the roof
over your head and the one thing
which will keep you alive

is the grey wool coat you bought me,
swathing me from collar to ankles,
the one I'm wearing now ...

Blizzard's lashing in our faces,
up our sleeves. The sea, the colour of unfathomed
ice, creaks and moans and

drowns out thought other than this one:
how long can you withstand
such cold? But the coat reaches

to its full height, snuggles us from the wind
which flays our lungs, frost-wraps
our limbs before it bites them off.

Huddling in a sheep's woolly kindness,
we'll nestle in this womb till morning.

My mother on the back of my chariot

Not once did you ask me
   to slow down
urge me to be careful
    as we approached
a crossing
     leaned into
a bend. Mounted
    on the back
of my gilded bicycle
     you rode with me
along the rutted flat
   of narrow paths
and unploughed stretches
    up effortless
hills
     onto tree-
lined streets
where houses flitted past
   at a window
a face you might
once have known but
   remembering
didn't feel important
   here now
soaring with me
    through these billowing
   fields
the green
tide coursing
    salty to
the bay and

everywhere
    we breathed
        the sky
            the wheels of
        blue air
    moving
under streaked grey
    light tossed
your flying span of years
    you felt safe
    and held tight

My mother's courage tape

Also stowed on that tape in the car glove-pocket,
Placido Domingo, Pavarotti –
I can hear them fortify your soul
with courage or if not courage then the kind
of bravura that goes with keeping on
through winter, both hips on the blink
and no one special enough to share your bed
or your crossword puzzle.

But what was it with that song by Jimmy Nail?
crocodile shoes ... crocodile shoes ...
you'd never wear such things yourself –
skin flayed from a croc and polished supple.
So it must have been the tune, or was it the phrase
on the clarinet, that line where he calls those shoes
his only friends – which struck a chord with you
saving your red Ferragamos for one last flush?

And you'd have taken him under your wing –
this fellow in Jimmy's song, who *soaked
through with rain,* having *lost so much
in such short time,* still steps into his most
extravagant pair, kept meticulously shoe-tree'd
in an ill-lit cupboard.

The broomcycle

for Samuel

Years on,
he liked to tell his friends
how she rode at such
amazing speeds,
die Haare fliegend.
Even at the age of nine
he'd climb on behind her
and they'd zip through streets,
weave in and
out of traffic,
glide past lights already
turning amber.
Soon they were lifting
above the roofs,
the sycamores, the park strewn
with conkers, soaring
over the shop
that sold liquorice
and his favourite loaf
baked *mit Kümmel
und Honig.*
Rain on their skin,
car fumes, wood-smoke,
the crackle of leaves,
black wind flocks swirling.

Lair

I swaddled my children in the cleft of a cave
above a pool filled with blind fish, air-borne spiders
skimming the walls – left them there –
as if they were troglobites ...
What desperate errand was I on?
where the father? A hundred passageways
is what I find when I return –
but which will take me to my infants
now the tide is smashing in?

Or is this the moment of dreaming when the heart
refuses one more step into the chasm
of nightmare? when it flails back towards
the light of home, the accommodating
shapes, the hub of choices. What sort of woman
tucks her children into a basket of rock
at the mouth of the sea? where the only sense
is to run harder from the thunder
crashing at her heels ...

But this is where rescue intervenes –
switches off the waves,
hauls up the children,
points the trio to safe ground.
Our house stands under a row of trees,
my children grown hale, their mother still searching
for a language to describe the dangers
from which the heart has to flee;
the terror of the cave where love is enacted.

Dance to your daddie

      see how she's managed
      to turn the tap
      fill the kettle
      by stretching
         on tiptoe

      swirled warm water
      around the pot
      added
two teaspoonfuls
      of Yorkshire,
        shakily pours
          the boiling liquid
brew for two minutes
      now she strains
        the leaves
      in a dented sieve
plenty of milk
three sugars
      grips the saucer
      with both hands
         scalding drink
          lapping
        bridling
    at the rim

      her back rigid
      till she sets
      it down

      on the polished
      surface
         for you

Whenever the van pulls up

For weeks my father thrashed the animal
to make it heel –
unruly dogs must be broken.

Aunt Irene often told us how their old man
took a belt to his son,
who then enlisted at sixteen

as soon as war broke out.
The ghost of a whipped boy
walked the house of my father.

My mother, pleading with him to stop,
slowly conceded to the mercy
of having the creature put down.

But still, years later, that van pulls up:
she makes a soundless lurch towards the rap at the door

and the boxer quivers, his coat rippling sheeny
as before a beating.

My father has already left for work
so my mother is alone when

the stricken eyes beg
one last time for reprieve ...

Then the van drives off.

On this mid June morning,
a breeze lapping in from the sea
she doesn't go for a walk.

The upholstered stage

>   … on and on I sing – either
> he's listening or he's not.

From the grey upholstery of his new Ford – he in his suede
gloves and watching the road – I strive to reach
the crystal notes, high octave chorus sweeping upwards
from the naked branches of sycamore and elm. On and on I go,
projecting my fledgling heart out to the stalls
as if I knew each escapade of yearning.

I took his silence as attention, acquiescence beyond
his usual bearing. Casting off our bodies, we were bigger than me,
bigger than him, moving like shadows against love's backdrop. Almost.

His mind is crumbling now –
>   hour by hour.

Is he, behind that raw-boned face, listening for a song
to carry him off beyond the darkening house,
the ravening tides? He slides his hand along the brim
of his hat, lifts his coat from the peg in the hall. Best hurry –
the engine's started – trees lilt by, house lights flare on
like rows and rows of breath-fanned candles.

Hello Daddy

But to return to the house:
         you walking up the path –
wearing dun raincoat, a buff trilby –
towards the front door.

In your presence, we're afraid to speak
until we've gauged your mood.

The light churns with interrupted weather,
shadows slipping through the air,
disturbing the water of the lily pond.

What is it you want from your bevy
of daughters? We wear your wide jaw,
your firm shoulders, and never discover the you.

We still retain a few versions, King Billy
is one: master at chess, louring at table yet
first to pour us snifters of wine.
Or old Father William who allowed three questions.

But to return to the house – the flowers
darken. On the tips of the grass, breeze
sways heavy, a disembodied voice
in search of language.

At the start of the crazy paving
that wends to the front door,
every day the gate
         lurches open

Slippage

Gaunt, he was still walking strong-bodied
down a corridor lined
with doctors, nurses.

But in the snapshot he's running
back up a beach, washed clean with salt,
ocean dripping between his shoulders,
down his chin.

Later, pouring drink into tumblers, the picnic
spread out on a tartan rug,
he's half erased
by a freight of shadow.

My mother's sleeping under her straw hat
when he re-enters the surf, bouldered
each side and caterwauling with seabirds,
the day slipping fast into the water.

The blown nest

I was twelve and mesmerised by her fingers
cradling a sparrow fledgling shaken from its nest
in the buffeted garden:

wind and rain clacketting the house,
our father's newspaper dropped
to the floor.

Now, I give my half-sisters – abandoned
when their mother fled four years on
in father's car –

this image of their mismatched parents
caught in a lull
brought on by outer turmoil. He, contained

by the drama of storm-light framed inside
the dormer window, his left leg slung over
the arm of his wide chair,

she, pregnant, newly his third wife,
sat opposite on the gold-braid sofa,
proffering warmed milk from her soft mouth:

her feel for feathery down,
minute wing-bones.

The seasoned dancer

There you were, in your frailness,
we not knowing what it is to hold you:
tentative the hand that seeks your hand,
the whittled curve of your thin shoulder.

No matter how little we flicker through your thoughts,
are there not ghosts who wear our likeness
in patterns of recurring music sighing from the dark?

Now for the first time your lip trembles –
oh to lift you up onto the light-spun boards
of the seasoned ship listing through gale force
as the mirrorball spins …

forties band, your favourite crooners,
luminescent silks and flow,
would we not glide across that floor,
swept up in the endless dance?

The longest hold

You used to lie on your stomach on the carpet
while we tickled you with a feather around your ears,
your shut eyes, your neck, your nostrils.
Sixpence if we made you laugh.

Now, no one had thought to clip your nails –
so I placed the old manicure set beside me
on the coffee table, settled your first hand
on my knees – fingers delicate as a pianist's

dancing over keys in a silent room nobody had noticed,
least of all you. What abuse you'd have unleashed
on such a poofta's calling, yet
Rachmaninov pleased you well enough.

And here the clean white moons I'd always remember.
Gently I snipped. It took a long time – the longest
I'd ever dared hold you.

This was the quietest we would be, in the wordless
fellowship of disregarded love that went back years
and had almost flourished in the unseeing dark.

Sixpence if I can make you laugh in this Chapel of Rest …
my finger a feather, I stroke your eyebrows.

The word for father

1

As you lay in your coffin, I slipped my book
inside your blazer. Plenty of time at last

for you to skim or hover at some particular page,
the underside of words like maps of shadows

sketching the curve of an abandoned country.
Even in the homelier nouns, such as *greenhouse*,

armchair, *spade* or *lawnmower*, can you hear the path
fork into absence where neither of us speaks

the other's name? Yet we wear the shapes
of our connection with its smell of something

burning on the stove, stirred with resin breeze
from the fir at the window.

A furnace of letters, fire-winged,
commingling with your silted flesh.

Is this the place where we might finally meet?

...

2

From time to time I hear you exclaim:
Ye gods, lass, where's the rhyme in these poems?
Only now do I learn about your fondness
for language, the OED spread open on the desk
in your former office, your *con'troversy*
versus *contro'versy* with clients.

Watching from your last days
at the window, you rescued
from your crumbling brain
      slipstream

  the airy sibilance of birds
    swooping – wind and sea
swelling the climate of your tongue –
   wheeling sky combing
     the broken currents.

A night scene

Just like a fifties film: fire churning
in the grate, her family in their gilded frames
watching from the cluttered mantelpiece,
roses stirring in the fireside rug ...
    Pan to her father suddenly stood
at the bed saying: 'Wake up! The police are here' –
bundling her, she's maybe seven,
into her woollen dressing-gown, hauling
her downstairs to two plain clothes policemen.
She can't stop trembling.
And instead of the language the heart
seeds as it rustles slowly
like a tree fanned by birds and winding
breezes of stars,
she's made to answer raw:
'Did she let do to her those things
scrawled on the wall for her father
to read coming late home?'

She can still feel their eyes hacking open
a path, trying to lure badness
in and bad acts, fear wheedling her dazed
thoughts: maybe in sleep she'd grown
a different self who disappeared in the bushes
with those men who skulked well beyond
reach of her mother's voice fetching her in
before perils of dark-fall. In the film she never finds
her way back: besmirched by the thrust
of their regard, how it tries to flush out
shadows from her hair, clammy thumb-prints
from her skin. Her words prised open to receive guilt.

A sex doll

She'd never tell which marauding gang of kids out after dark,
had hurt her more, betrayed her kindness.

Or had some lonely romantic dumped her here
to take her chances on the tide?

The thought of what cloyed her: the holes,
bruises, the murky sea – I knew

these things from dreams. From lives.
Almost I think of lifting her out,

mollying her in warm pyjamas after carrying
her home – if I could only wash off

the slimy suspicion of her body rigged
with low-rent sensation and what if her eyes

flinch or I catch her breathing the stifled moans
of whoever used her? How could I trust her

not to sully my sheets, murder at the bedroom door
the intimacies of my best angel?

So I leave her to the waves plaiting her hair
with green-snot bows of seaweed.

If on the stairs

Nothing really happened.
A whiff of coal laid fresh on the grate,
hovering in her nightgown   a friend's
daughter when the others were gone up to dress

rosebud womanbaby fondlechild –
unexplored beyond forbidden
crossing   don't let her
tell   how once   a shadow locked
inside a shadow   slipped in
through the door   up through the hall
of a winding   leading to
a winding
         no light   no air
from what was never heeded
till I   the lamb   was unhinged
by an urge   a murky
flower   still I search her eyes to know
what memory   she wields.

>   … … I'd have let go   I'd have let
>   go those bleak
>   petals   even if
>   there'd been no
>   others opening cupboards,
>   slamming drawers –
>   if there'd been no rustle on the stairs

57

The tree

In the winding
near-deserted
lanes at dusk
how will we comfort

the Great Fretted Moths
searching in their liminal silks
for the echo
of branches –

if we drive out every place
where the Tree
bends its voice
into the cotils?

every gap in the walls
or stone latch
where leaves
scatter

into our stymied thoughts
their green cadences
of rustling
air.

When we sleep
the open
vowels
of landscape still draw

us back
to the windswept oak
the fissured bole
of language.

cotil: Jersey-speak (Jerriase) for a steep plot of land

The angel

The first time I saw him
was from the side window
of José's taxi:

about 3 metres tall and strung
from a steel frame,
he grieves for the men

who died building roads, blasting
through volcanic rock, hauling
explosives along sheer levadas.

Head down, knees
crooked – poised
to dive. An angel plunged

from grace. Imagine how
the shattered souls
falling in multi-coloured pieces,

had stunned him,
casting him
deathwards

among the smithereens of lives
he'd grown too fond of …
cleft between angel

realm and the tendernesses,
irritations which day by day
had whittled his wings.

The next time I saw him, a teenage biker
was keeling in a slow
skid –

into near-amputation, paralysis,
debris. Saved
by the angel's grassy verge.

The boy told us he'd heard
a strange language of vowels
as tall as polished windows overlooking

the banana groves,
the gardens of marrows
shot through with winding

breakneck roads, broken hills,
arteries of tunnels – all seen
through a haze of misshapen

weather: the overcast sea shuddering
with radiance, sky tremulous blue,
coursingly and sluggish. He knew

the place he could not get back to
with his heart divided
by this fractured landscape.

Terra Nova II

Beyond running water and parents,
we huddled around the old record player
like Scott and his crew warmed
by their gramophone,
its metallic crackle floating
across polar landscape.
Tomorrow we too would set out,
push our bodies to their limits.

Frightened of the haul,
our Siberian ponies, fleeces white against the radiance,
already kicked and whinnied.

> *Only now do we grasp the absence of landmarks,*
> *the force of the zero pulling us in with nothing*
> *to hold onto but words freezing over*
> *in our mouths, drifts of silence emptying*
> *of any whiff of the human.*
> *Numbed to the clamour of who we are,*
> *we trudge through the wind,*
> *scale glass-like breakers more blinding*
> *than desire; only to discover someone else*
> *has been there, peered down*
> *the chasm of the ice-bound self,*
> *hoisted his flag.*
>
> *And how to make our way back*
> *with dead fingers, feet blackened*
> *in swollen boots, how long to return*
> *from the bottom of the world?*

The motley jam-jars smudged with our prints,
slip through our hands.
How long before we're clinging to ice-floes?
trekking again across the waiting plains
whose mysteries will burst open
to the crunch of our footfalls.

Horse queen

… Penance of sugar,
crusts of bread –
I had wanted to abate
the sorrow of a deposed
Horse Queen.

Night trembles through her sweated flanks,
her lake-black eyes
still foraging for light,
she who muzzled once
my open palm.

What wouldn't I give to double
back through the woods …
undo the years I failed
to regale her with burnished
apples, polished oats.

Now her spirit, a cold wind,
rucks up my duvet –
I call out the names, the toll
of creatures I must carry with me
to a place of redress.

Bray

for Helen and Leile

According to Monsieur, who'd named him Oscar,
he could smell a storm brewing the midnight
at stroke of dawn. Daylight, he'd patrol
the pass, forage milky stems.

After climbing for weeks through a valley
of airy creatures lit like flares, the old exhaustions,
mid-sentence, creaked softly at a bend
in the road. Then, as we tiptoed beyond, so far

into the place of hooves and wings, light and water,
his voice was there to meet us at the crossroads
and bestow gifts on us: fresh longing enveloped
the hills, swaddled breezes and grew resistant to ever

going home to the humdrum shoring
of provisions, the day to day push
against grief. Yes, that and the boast,
the shameless triumph of a cranky god

who owns lust: *Je suis le Roi! Mon nom –
c'est Creon.* How hard it is to sing like this,
the trammelled heart rocked by violence
and still braying *here, yet here.*

Talking the cat to the vet

Has his bedroom talk ever grown as fond
as this mewling code of stretched
vowels and lapping sibilants? About to receive an annual jab,
she was threading a paw
through the wire hatch
to the thirty year old bloke standing on the edge
of love strayed too far
from its hallowed creatures.

Tawny-gold her sovereign fur and all of Egypt
watching from her face.
Yet no matter the freight of tenderness
the flesh carries within – as though there were a valley
or purring delta of the self tucked inviolable
behind a fold of breath –
the body sounds its minutes and hours.

Now he's promising her
she'll soon be home.

Angel ascending

Inside the window
on the first floor
stood a ladder
at a steep
gradient,
a makeshift
arrangement
to the top
of the house,
its sky-filled rooms.

One night we'd folded
away our clothes,
slipped into bed,
he always naked,
when it occurs
to him he'd forgotten
something,
so up he jumps,
flicks on
the hall light,
climbs bare
the ladder.

They who chanced
to glance out
will have pinched themselves
to check
they weren't dreaming
the window
illumined
with his celestial body:
such radiant
calves, thighs,
ah those heavenly buttocks,
and, as he climbed
the rungs,
his tackle
swinging.

A pair of socks

His breathing swims our sea of pillows, flows level
as the tide swelling the salt-rock bays tonight.

Come morning, he'll minister to the sock drawer,
preside over strays: one nestles in the duvet,

another's flown into a tree, a sodden finch. With each retrieval
he'll ward off a loss, stall yet one more lonely prospect.

I hold his sex as if it were mine and this is how our touch
journeys through the dark of our most need,

the days, years of the neglected vigil of who we are.
Stars chime, we reverse our moorings, his hand listening

to the pulse of my left breast – among its chatter of dreams,
one shape still vibrant isn't snagged on the breeze.

Folds of our other selves prepare to dress
for daytime, choosing from the fresh-sorted

laundry a pair entwined … now caressed
over the toes, the arch, the heel –

each one drawn singly.

A stack of blue-glazed bowls

Does the history of breaking
outdo the mend?

Does a careless hand, at large
among the glass, outweigh

the painstaking manoeuvres to stow
our rose-patterned cups inside a draughty kitchen?

What if lopped-off handles,
smithereens of china were to block

our entrance to rooms where we touch,
where we furnish one another against the spills

and blows for which we're ill-equipped
to pan and salvage on hands and knees?

Each day in our fragile habitation
we stack sea-green plates on wobbly shelves.

Nights, if we've avoided damage,
we lie here in the dark, windows open,

honouring the shape of our chipped house
standing under the trees, the rusting gutter primed
to catch each trickle of pearled light.

The sliding hills

He told himself he had to stand against the wind,
absorb the commotion of the hills.
When that didn't work, he strained to lean
closer to the centre of the sliding valley.
He knew now what he must do:
risk his balance to the storm, the rain-mired
paving stones, offer the full extent
of his body and pluck, without trampling
the beds, a last wild strawberry,
Fragaria vesca of the soul, its pulp
meshed in seed and quivering.

Now I bind his brokenness,
his mind shaken up by weather
that won't lie flat until the house is gutted,
books churning in the currents,
kettle boiling on the convulsing tide. So if this is the fall
below the shoreline, what I ask
is to *please, please* draw from the pith
of my own mending, one more steadying
act of love, a holding kiss to go out on.

Muses of the shower room

They're there behind the shower curtain,
giving off headiness of rose, the calm
of geranium mingled with salt of a fresh swim.

Snuck under the bra of a tankini is a seaweed tendril. What more
to say? Yet still they shadow the quiet of distance:
when I'm going for a pee or standing on a chair

to fix a light bulb, they insist on holding to the subject
of how the tide has reached the shingle line, dusk breezing
into the bay, asking only that the waves break at the edge

of consonance, that vowels be bestowed with the soughing
quality of the near-drowned. Of syntax they desire
an expansiveness, a oneness between body

of text and their own fluent strokes.
What if I can't convey the rocky escarpments, shifting
light and breaking surfaces? Or if I fail

in the sludge between words to suggest the power
of the submerged narrative: love's losses
and growing old? Will they pursue me until the work

is done; until they, untouched by winter approaching,
bask in the shored-up waters of the page?
But I hear them now – emerging from the sea and heading

for the shower room … trailing their towels along the sand-
swilled floor! Yes, I can feel the pummelling all down
their spines, taste the fragrance lapping their silhouettes.

By the same author

The Usher's Torch (Hearing Eye, 2005)   £7.00

Hearing Eye
Box 1, 99 Torriano Avenue, London, NW5 2RX
email: books@hearingeye.org
www.hearingeye.org